Praise for *The B*

W9-AZG-224

"If you are a teenager within a divorced family, this book will give you clear advice about divorce, from the emotional adjustment to the importance of not triangulating yourself in between your parents, as well as practical advice about travel, communication, stepparents, friends, where to seek support, who to trust, and much more."

—Dr. Schlomit Gross

Dr. Schlomit Gross is a clinical psychologist specializing in child and family therapy, in practice for over twenty-five years.

"*The Bright Side* is a must-read for all whose parents are divorced. Max Sindell has used his considerable experience as a child and teenager to create an articulate, friendly, practical, and empowering guide for how to survive and even thrive in a divorced family."

—Dr. Allan Gold

Dr. Allan Gold has been working with children as the district psychologist for the Reed School District in Marin County for nearly twenty-nine years.

"The book is well written, lively, and fun to read. It contains lots of useful information. The Bill of Rights is clever and well put."

—Andrew Cherlin, Ph.D.

Andrew Cherlin is a professor of sociology at Johns Hopkins University. Over the last thirty-five years, he has published articles on many topics relating to the sociology of the family, particularly in the area of divorce and remarriage.

Surviving Your
Parents' Divorce

The
BRIGHT
SIDE

Max Sindell

Health Communications, Inc.
Deerfield Beach, Florida

www.hcibooks.com

Library of Congress Cataloging-in-Publication Data

Sindell, Max.

The bright side : surviving your parents' divorce / Max Sindell.

   p. cm.

   ISBN-13: 978-0-7573-0625-9 (trade paper)

   ISBN-10: 0-7573-0625-X (trade paper)

   1. Children of divorced parents—Life skills guides. I. Title.

HQ777.5.S535 2007

306.89—dc22

                               2007012744

Publisher: Health Communications, Inc.
               3201 S.W. 15th Street
               Deerfield Beach, FL 33442-8190

Cover design by Larissa Hise Henoch
Inside book design and formatting by Dawn Von Strolley Grove

CONTENTS

CONTENTS

CONTENTS

A Note to Kids Only

Hi!

This book is for you, not your parents. This whole process you're going through is tough. Believe me, I know. I've been there. Divorce ran in my family even before I was born. My parents were divorced when I was six. I've had multiple stepparents, stepbrothers, and half-brothers, a lot of which you're probably going to have sometime, maybe soon. It's all so confusing, trying to figure out how to deal with hundreds of new situations and how to keep everything straight. It's easy to forget where you stand in the world.

My stepfather used a very interesting metaphor once. I was trying so hard to make both my parents happy that I was miserable myself. He said to me, "You are the star of your own movie. Everyone else is just a supporting character. If someone is in your movie and they're not supporting you, they get fired. But also remember that you're not the star of anyone else's movie." When I feel overwhelmed, this advice helps me keep things in perspective.

You may not think you need any help. And you might not. But in any case, I believe that at least a couple of things in here will help you out and make your life a little easier. Divorce is a mixed bag, and it's easy to get overwhelmed with the huge changes that are taking place in your life. With many changes and disruptions, it gets easy to focus on everything that's going wrong and everything you think you've lost. But this book isn't about that. When I went through my experiences with divorce, I was lucky enough to have my parents, brothers, and stepparents all help me with good advice. They helped me see the bright side of all these new experiences, and they helped me keep a level head and a positive perspective. In this book, I've tried to put together the most important stuff I was taught, to try and make this whole thing a little easier for you to deal with. So take a look—it's not that long. It should only take you a little while to read.

About Me

The divorce your parents are going through and the experience you are having are totally unique; they're bound to provide you with plenty of challenges that will be entirely your own. I can't possibly claim to know everything you're going through right now because I don't know your story. But if you don't mind, I'd like to share mine with you. If you don't really care about my story, that's fine too. Skip ahead to the Divorced Kids' Bill of Rights, and see if that makes some sense. For now, let me tell you about what happened to me:

Before I was even born, my family was pretty complicated. My father married his first wife when they were still in college together in Ohio. Over the course of ten years, they moved from Cleveland to Los Angeles to France and back to L.A., during which time they had three sons: Josh, the oldest; Milo, two years younger than Josh; and David, eight years younger than Milo. By the time David was born, my father's first marriage had started to fall apart. When David was two, my father, age thirty-six, had met my mother, age twenty-four, and they moved in together with all three boys, now ages twelve, ten, and two. For the next several years, the boys spent most of their time with my father and mother. My mother and my brothers became very close, but she still wanted a child of her own. And so, a few months before David turned eight, I was born.

For the first five years of my life, things were awesome. All six of us lived together, and I got to spend a lot of time with my half-brothers in the house. No one ever called them that, however. I grew up with them as my brothers, and that's never changed.

Anyway, as we've all figured out, not all marriages last forever, and when I was six, my parents separated. Both my grandfathers died, one grandmother got Alzheimer's, and the other fell off a roof and broke her back. It felt like everything bad that could happen, did.

I went through what someone clinical might refer to as "a low point." The next couple of years felt like I was shuffled from hospital to hospital and then from household to household, while my parents yelled at each other about anything and everything they could find to disagree on, most of it about me. When a marriage splits, there are usually only one or two reasons for the couple to ever communicate again: money and children. Of course, the arguments about children are often arguments about money anyway.

That was the worst part of it all when I was younger. Whenever my parents fought, they either fought about me or money, and I was never allowed to be a part of either conversation. Looking back, I guess it makes sense. I mean, I was six or seven, and I don't think my parents wanted me around during custody or child support battles. On the other hand, being shuttled around and having my schedule decided for me without my input was enormously frustrating. Growing up, my parents had always encouraged me to be as mature as possible as fast as possible, but when there was a situation that I thought I'd have a chance to prove myself in, I was left totally out of it. So while I view that early exclusion as unfortunately necessary, I desperately wanted to make my voice heard.

Shortly after the divorce, most of those problems were solved for me when my father decided to move away to Colorado and I could only see him during my vacations from school. No question, it was a weird experience to have my father halfway across the country, and I missed him when he was gone. I also missed having a house with all my brothers in it, but their moving out was inevitable; David was already fifteen and hadn't lived with his mother full-time in over ten years.

But there was a flip side to all of this, and that flip side was independence. Life became enormously exciting because I was allowed to do things like fly halfway across the country by myself. My father moved to a small town, gave me free rein, and I put four hundred miles on my bike that first summer.

Shortly after my parents divorced, I was introduced to one of the most awkward circumstances I've ever had to deal with: parental dating. I was pretty lucky though, and my mom quickly found a new husband whom I approved of, and my stepfather and I have since become very close. I can't imagine my life without him in it.

At the same time, across the country my father was meeting new women, and after a few years he moved in with a girlfriend who eventually became my first stepmother. My parents both have pretty decent taste when it comes to significant others, and I grew very close to my first stepmother as well. My stepparents had strong influences on my childhood, and I'm thankful that they did. I know not everyone is lucky enough to have the experience I had, and I'll have more to say about that later on, but this story isn't quite finished.

While my dad had lived in Colorado, my mother and my stepfather decided it was time to leave Los Angeles, and we moved up to the San Francisco Bay Area shortly before I began the fifth grade. This was an adjustment I found even harder to make than my parents' divorce, and it took me a while to stop being miserable. I found it tough to make new friends and find people I could trust, and for a little while I felt pretty alone.

When I advanced to sixth grade, my father left Colorado and came to San Francisco to be closer to me, much to my mother's dismay. My parents still weren't getting along, but they managed to hammer out a schedule for me where I only saw my father every other weekend. My parents didn't want to disrupt my life too much, but it was frustrating having my father across the bay but only seeing him for three out of every fourteen days.

I started to get really fed up with being left out of deciding how my life was run and where my time was spent, and I ended up doing the unthinkable: I went and talked to my school counselor. It turned out to be one of the best decisions I ever made.

I have to say, school counselors get a bad rap. I know that sometimes they try and tell you to do things like "talk your problems over" with some jerk who kicks your seat in Spanish class when what you really want to do is pop him one in the mouth, but they're just there to help you. More importantly, when it comes to situations where you feel too small to be listened to, they can be a powerful voice on your side. I'll talk more about that later.

Anyway, I told my counselor that I was tired of being left out of the decisions that affected my life; I was too afraid that if I said anything, my parents wouldn't listen to me. With his help, however, we put together a meeting with both my parents where I presented to them the schedule that I wanted. My parents agreed, and once I proved that my schedule worked, I was given the freedom to plan out my own time with each parent.

I should have known, of course, that being able to plan my own schedule didn't necessarily mean that my life would get any easier. Instead of my parents fighting with each other about which holiday I would spend with whom, they'd argue about it with me. My stress level went up, but I definitely preferred being in control of my own schedule and life.

By the time I made it to high school, my dad was in the process of getting divorced from his third wife. It was tough, but I also knew it would be better for the both of them.

A few years later, about the time I got fed up with my high school and went to boarding school, my father married my second stepmother, another wonderful addition to my family. My mother and stepfather are still very happily married and just celebrated their twelfth wedding anniversary. And as for me, I'm fresh out of college and getting ready for the next stage of my life.

I hope you're still reading, and that at least a little bit of that sounded familiar. Like I said, no two divorces are the same, and I know because I can tell you that firsthand. But I'm tired of talking about me, me, me. Let's start talking about you.

Part 1

Relating to Your Parents and Other Adults

The Divorced Kids' Bill of Rights

It seems like everyone has a Bill of Rights these days. All Americans have one in their Constitution. The Geneva Convention has a Bill of Rights for prisoners of war. And if you Google "Bill of Rights," well, it looks like just about everybody has one: doctors' patients, children, goldfish, gerbils. . . . The point is, I think kids with divorced parents deserve a Bill of Rights too. In this section, you'll find some basic rights that you have with your family and that your parents should respect.

Read over them, think about them, and sit down with your parents and tell them to read them too. Share them with your parents early on and discuss them together, and start figuring out how they are going to make sure they respect these inalienable rights.

I. THE RIGHT TO BE SAFE AND FEEL SAFE

The most important thing in a divorce with kids is that they feel safe and secure. That means saying something if you're home alone too much, if a relative or stepparent says something to you that isn't right, or if they treat you in a way that makes you uncomfortable. If there ever is a time you don't feel safe, tell your parents, and if you can't tell them, tell a counselor or tell a friend. This is your most important right.

II. THE RIGHT TO AWARENESS

You have a right to know what's going on. Your parents should not lie to you or hide the truth from you about anything to do with you. This does not mean, however, that they have to tell you everything. Some things should remain private between your parents until you are older, and until they feel they want to tell you. For instance, they don't have to reveal to you the intimate details of their arguments about child support. But if they're having a discussion about your schedule, you have the right to know and to make your voice heard.

III. THE RIGHT TO COUNSELING

Divorce can be very disempowering. It can make you feel like you don't have a say and don't make a difference, and that's exactly where a counselor comes in. A counselor should be someone whom you can talk to privately, without your parents there, and who can help you with your situation.

When I was eleven, I'd had enough with my parents' problems, and I met with my middle school counselor, Dr. Gold. We talked once a week or so about how I felt concerning my parents' situation, and he helped me realize that I have a voice that my parents should hear. Without him, I don't think I would have had my say until I was older. He was instrumental in helping me tell my parents how I felt and getting them to respect my opinion.

School counselors are not the only people you can talk to. Adult friends of the family who are unbiased, or the parents of good friends of yours, are also good people to talk to.

All of this brings up an important issue. If you are ever harmed or threatened in any way, or you don't feel safe with a parent, the most important thing you can do is to talk to someone who can help you. Above everything else is Right Number I: The right to be safe and to feel safe. Remember that.

IV. THE RIGHT TO BE HEARD

Sometimes, when your parents are trying to sort out what they think is best for you, they can forget to listen to the most important person: You! Sometimes, you know what you need better than they do, and they'll forget to ask. If you can't get them to listen to you by yourself, it's important to have someone—a counselor or a friend—talk for you. That way you can make sure that you have a say, and that your parents really know what you need.

V. THE RIGHT TO BE YOUR OWN PERSON

Before your parents were divorced, there was you, your mom, your dad, and the other people in your family. The same is true now. Your parents have to respect your right to feel the way you feel.

Your parents will very likely start dating after they are divorced. This is normal. I've seen my father date and marry twice after my parents split. Trust me, you'll get used to it. But with all of that comes the fact that you are not a tool for your parents to get dates.

In dealing with stepparents, or the people your parents are

dating, your rights stand. They are still in effect. It's important to set boundaries with your parents' friends. You must tell both your parents and their friends when those boundaries are crossed. If those boundaries are crossed in a major way, and you don't feel safe, tell a counselor. Plain and simple.

VI. THE RIGHT TO BE NEUTRAL

Your parents, more likely than not, will argue about things when they get divorced. Again, this is normal. They will fight, and they might even say things about each other that aren't so nice. Sometimes, they may tell you about these things and ask you how you feel about them.

The long and the short of it is that you don't have to say a thing. You have the right, first of all, to not hear any of it. If you don't want to hear about how they feel about each other, then you don't have to. Tell them to stop, tell them you don't want to hear it. If they don't stop, leave and tell someone else.

Also remember that you never have to choose sides. I found it interesting and very informative to hear how my mother felt about my father and vice versa. I learned a lot from it. I learned that if I acted like either parent in a way that reminded the other of the reason they got divorced, they'd get angry really fast, which was a good thing to know. Regardless of all of that, the important thing is that you don't have to take a side with either parent. Be Switzerland. Stay neutral.

VII. THE RIGHT TO PRIVATE COMMUNICATION

You can say anything to anyone, without worrying about someone else listening. This means that if you want to be on the phone, then you can ask your parent to leave the room. That means you can write e-mails without your parent over your shoulder. That means that when you meet with a counselor or friend, you have privacy, unless you want your parent(s) there.

For the rest of your young adult life, I think you'll find these rights to be a useful guide for knowing where you stand and for knowing what you have to put up with and what you don't.

Who Made This Mess?

I'm sure that you've already had people tell you that the divorce isn't your fault. Your parents probably told you. Your parents' friends probably told you. Any counselor will tell you the same thing. Some guy on the street probably told you. Well, you know what? They're right.

In my house, the policy was that if you made a mess, you cleaned it up. That was the rule when I was six years old and sixteen years old. Now your parents have made what some would call a mess. And you don't have to clean it up, because it isn't your mess: It's theirs.

I don't have to tell you how hard it can be for two people to get along—sometimes, your biggest fights are with your best friend. And it can be difficult to keep a friendship close for ten or fifteen years, let alone a whole lifetime. There is any number of reasons why your parents decided they didn't want to be together anymore. They could have simply stopped getting along or found that they could no longer trust each other. Sometimes, the behavior of one parent can be dangerous, like an addiction to alcohol or drugs. But no matter what, be absolutely clear and don't flatter yourself: This isn't about you. The reasons or causes of the divorce are *their* problems, and not yours. Trust me, you're going to have enough to deal with without having to think about why your parents aren't married anymore.

Part 2

Family Politics

An Introduction to Politics

D ivorce brings along its own set of situations and scenarios, and it's important to know how to navigate those waters by knowing what to say and who to say it to. But I don't want you to get the impression that family politics, or even politics in general, is just about telling people what they want to hear.

Politics is an important part of everyday life. Knowing what to say and who to say it to is essential in dealing with people in every situation. For example, if your friend who happens to be sensitive about her weight comes in to your house wearing tight pants that don't fit very well, the wrong thing to say would be, "Wow, those make you look *huge!*"

I know that has nothing to do with families, but bear with me. Family politics can be really tricky, and it's tough to balance the wants and needs of everyone who's going to be placing demands and responsibilities on you, or sharing information that could be considered controversial. Also, realize that a lot of people don't think about these things the way you do, and they may not realize how what they say affects you. There might be certain times of the day you're grumpier or more tired than others, or there might be certain topics, about your family or anything else, that easily get you angry or hurt. While it's difficult to stay on the high road sometimes, do your best to let that stuff go. If they didn't mean it, try to hint or explain directly why you were hurt or bothered by what someone said. If, unfortunately, you think someone said something just to get under your skin, don't do anything. The last thing you want to give them is the satisfaction of knowing they got to you. There's a ton of little things to worry about when it comes to parental politics, and the next few sections are all about the politics of families and friends.

Your Conduct and Being a Conduit

It is likely, maybe inevitable, that your conduct with each of your parents will have to change a little bit, because their conduct with each other is changing dramatically. At some point, your parents may not want to discuss an issue between each other, for whatever reason, and your mother will give you a message to relay to your father, or vice versa.

Now comes an important choice of whether you become that conduit for information between your parents or let them handle their own affairs. Don't worry too much about it, because in reality you can always change your mind. But if you want to, you can serve as a conduit for your parents. Of course, this role comes with enormous responsibilities, pressures, and stresses. However, the benefit is that it gives you a lot of control over what is going on in your own life and keeps you in the know.

For example, from an early point in my parents' divorce, it became obvious that they really hated talking to each other unless they absolutely had to. I saw my opportunity, and I offered to make both their lives a little easier. For the next decade or so, I relayed most of the information between my parents. This allowed me to make my own schedule, to know about and have an opinion on what they were arguing over, and to lead a generally more informed life.

Most of the time, this was great, but sometimes I dreamed about what my life would be like without all the stress that comes with being a conduit. If I had chosen not to, they would have taken care of a lot of stuff without me, which would have alleviated a lot of my stress. But then I'd see them fighting all the time, they'd be angrier at one another, and I'd have a lot less of a say in how my life was run. I chose to be informed and deal with the stress that comes with it. Both options are valid, and the choice is up to you.

In the following sections, I'll discuss a few of the situations you might have to deal with and suggest how to deal with them as best as possible.

Insults

Chances are that your parents aren't feeling particularly rosy about each other right now. This is, of course, normal. They may also revert to something you saw on the playground in third grade: insults and name-calling. My parents acted this way once in a while, and I told them I didn't want to hear it. If you don't want to hear it, tell them to stop. If they don't stop, leave. By now you should know how to defend yourself if you're feeling powerless. Find someone to help you. If you ask your parents to stop insulting one another in front of you and they don't, get a counselor to help you.

Another word of caution: It's not necessarily a good idea to take any one parent's side, especially during one of their tirades about the other. If you stand there and nod your head, your parent might use your agreement as evidence or use you as a wedge to back up his or her opinion the next time they talk to your other parent. Remember, it's your right not to be used as a bargaining chip, so make sure you stay neutral and that your parents respect your neutrality. Even if you *do* agree with what your parent is saying, it's best to stay out of it. You don't want to end up pushing either parent away.

On the other hand, if you're the curious type, then by all means listen with open ears to what your parents have to say about each other's behavior. If you choose to, there are two things I would *not* recommend. First, don't repeat *anything* you hear. Period. Second, and this is important: Don't get stuck trying to defend one of your parents while the other is on a tirade about what a jerk the other one is. That's a very unhappy place to be.

Keeping Households Separate

I made this mistake all the time, and I still do, so I wanted to devote a section just to this. What I mean by keeping households separate is not coming back from your dad's house to your single mother and talking all through dinner about how cool your father's new girlfriend is. Or don't go to your dad's apartment and talk about how nice your mom's new BMW is that your stepfather just bought her. Stuff like that.

Sometimes, when you're looking for things to talk about, or experiences to share, those things just come out. Your parents want to hear about what's going on in your life, and you want to tell them. It happens. But when you're looking for things to share with either parent, there's one topic that they will *never* get tired of hearing about—you. Your parents love you more than anything, and they love hearing about you, no matter what. You are always a safe topic with your parents. The older you get, the less you'll want to say and the more they'll want to hear, but indulge them a little bit. The only reason they keep asking is because they love you. At least that's what I tell myself at the end of a stressful day taking midterms when my mom calls and wants to know how I'm enjoying my homework.

Home Is Where . . .

What is "home" anyway? That used to be an easy question, right? It was where you lived, with your parents. Of course, that definition doesn't really hold anymore. Sometimes it's hard not to have that one home. But that doesn't mean you don't have a home now.

For me, home is the place that makes me feel comfortable, safe, and at ease. The trick is being able to make yourself comfortable wherever you find yourself. It's not going to be an easy transition to make. There was one summer where I'd been away from my mother for almost three months. I was about nine, and I missed her more than anything. I called her crying on the phone that I wanted to come home, even though I had a flight in less than two weeks.

Another time I was away at boarding school, listening to the Beatles, when I realized that I was never going to be able to go home again. I mean, sure, I could always visit, but I'd never live there the way I had when I'd been a kid. I was sixteen, and I cried for hours that night.

That's normal. It's hard to be away from home, especially when, for the last eight years of your life, "home" has been in different cities and states simultaneously.

The reality is this: you're going to feel at home where you let yourself feel at home. At some point, home isn't going to be where your mom lives, where your dad lives, or the house that you grew up in. Home is going to be wherever *you* live, whether it's your mom's apartment, your dad's condo, or your dorm room at school. I have close friends and family all over the country, and I have lived at school in Michigan and Maryland. As long as I am with people I care about, I'm home. I hope you can feel the same way.

Two Houses, Both Alike in Dignity

Fact: You will never have all of your things in one place ever again. When your parents split, your stuff probably will too. Mom is going to live somewhere and Dad is going to live somewhere else, and a bunch of your stuff is probably going with each of them. This will be frustrating. The first and third Harry Potter books at Mom's, *Star Wars V* and *VI* at Dad's, and the homework due tomorrow morning fell out of your backpack in Dad's car on the way to Mom's house.

When I was little, before the divorce, I used to lose everything: sunglasses, disposable cameras, toothbrushes. Basically, if I could put it down somewhere, it wasn't safe. By the time my parents lived near each other in San Francisco, I'd been forced to develop a keen sense concerning the locations of all my belongings at all times. After being shuttled back and forth, first in L.A. and then back and forth to Colorado, I got sick of calling up one parent or the other and asking them to ship overnight whatever item I really needed for class that week. They got sick of it too.

There's no easy way to guarantee that you'll remember everything you need every time you go somewhere. No one's perfect.

The easiest way is to get two of everything you need. Get doubles of the basics: toothbrushes, toothpaste, shampoo, soap, underwear (take it from a college student, you can *never* have enough underwear), socks, pens, paper, things like that. The less stuff you have to carry back and forth, the better off you'll be.

In the event that you're going to be spending almost all your time with only one parent, this will be less of a problem. No matter what, you will still have to bring some things, like clothes, schoolwork, movies, books, or a laptop. So get a good bag you like and mark it well so it doesn't get lost. Use it as a base from house to house, but don't live out of it; you'll feel like a traveling salesman. Just keep the stuff in it that you know you'll need, and make sure that when you're done using the stuff, put it back in the bag. Making a checklist isn't a bad idea, depending on how paranoid you are about someone reading your stuff. Because your father won't be thrilled when he *has* to drive you to your mom's house at 11 PM because you forgot your American History textbook. He really won't be. Trust me.

Managing Your Time, 1

If you can, and you want to (that's most important), try to spend as much time as you can with each of your parents. And don't make your decision because Dad's house has better video games or Mom lets you eat junk food. Your parents are special people who have a lot to offer you, so just spend time with them.

Sometimes you won't want to be at one house because of some minor problem, like your bed at your mom's house is uncomfortable or your dad doesn't let you stay out past 10 PM. The easiest way to fix those problems is to *tell* your parents that there's a problem. If they don't know why you don't want to come over, they'll be hurt and assume that you don't want to be with them. They really just want to see you and to make sure that you're happy, and if you tell them what's wrong they'll probably do their best to fix it. But don't use those as excuses to make your parents jump through hoops just to please you. That's not right, and your parents will resent it after a while, and the last thing you want is your parents to resent you for using them. But they will do what they can to spend quality time with you because that's the thing they really want more than anything. Remember that.

Now, if there is ever a serious reason that you don't want to spend time with one parent or the other, and I really mean a serious reason, like you have a stepfather you always fight with and your mother doesn't do anything to help you, then it's time to go for outside help. You know what to do. Get in touch with a counselor who can help you get your voice heard.

If your parent lives far away, it doesn't mean they don't want to see you or talk to you all the time. So call them on the phone, or e-mail them, and tell them how your life is. They'll appreciate it more than you know.

Managing Your Time, 2

The first thing you'll notice that disappears along with your parents' marriage is going to be time. Time gets scarce for two reasons. The first reason is that a lot of your time is going to be spent traveling and communicating. Since everything isn't all in one place anymore, you'll be driving or flying from parent to parent, or on the phone with one or the other, talking about your day, making plans, packing, and unpacking.

The other reason is that your parents are going to both want time with you. And at most, if you keep it equal, no parent can have more than half of your time. Plus, as you get older, you're going to want more time for your friends or for yourself.

For my junior and senior years of high school, I chose to go to boarding school. It was a great school, and I loved it. A side benefit of all of it was that for most of the year, I didn't have to worry about splitting up my time. Most of those old battles disappeared, with a few notable exceptions: breaks. (If you don't go to boarding school, you won't escape this battle. Just wait until college.) I would come home and get less sleep than I did at school. A day with my mom, a day with my dad, a day with my friends, and a day for myself, and the cycle would start over again. In reality, it was more like a quarter of a day for each, split up all the time. Lunch at Dad's, dinner with Grandma, and tapping your foot impatiently until you're allowed to go hang out at your friend's house. I put about a thousand miles a week on my car when I'm home, just trying to see everyone.

The point of all this? Keep a calendar. Don't keep just one, keep three: one for you, one for your mom, one for your dad. Make sure you keep them coordinated and up to date at all times. When you're younger, it's more likely that your parents will be deciding your schedule for you, which is fine. You shouldn't have to worry about that stuff. But at some point, you'll be the one determining your own schedule, and with that comes the responsibility of keeping other people posted. A lot of that is just about making sure everyone's happy, so get used to it.

The truth is your parents will be absolutely thrilled to let you keep your own schedule *as long as you keep them informed*. The less they know, the more they think you're hiding information and the more suspicious they get. Make it easy for them and for yourself: let them know what's going on.

A quick note about making other people happy: it's not your job. In reality, it's impossible to make your friends, your parents, and yourself happy at all times. I guess I'm just saying, don't stress out over it too much. Make sure everyone knows that you're thinking about them, and do your best to split up your time in a way that works best for you. That's really it. Take care of yourself. Remember, you are the star of your own movie.

Talking the Talk

All this scheduling just cannot work without proper communication. Remember Right VII: your right to communication. Your parents on each end need to keep in touch with you, and you need to keep in touch with them. You should have a phone in your room, or access to one where you can talk alone.

If you feel like all of your conversations end up being the same three or four sentences, try to think about what you're going to talk about beforehand. Make a little list of things you experienced that you want to share with them or something really cool that you learned, or just tell them about how you're feeling about a friend. I know it can seem really weird to talk to your parents about personal stuff, and even worse, sometimes they want to try to actually *do* something to help you. But even if you keep it very general, it's a good idea to let your parents know what kind of emotions you're going through, so they know how to talk to you. If they don't know how to talk to you, tell them flat out. If you don't want their advice and just want them to listen, tell them. If you want advice, ask. If you don't want to talk about school, tell them that too.

Don't forget, your parents are people too. Ask them about their day. Ask them about work, about what they're doing for fun, or ask them about what's going on in the world, whether it be the weather, politics, TV, or sports. What passions do you share with your parents? Do you both love biking, reading mysteries, or talking technology? At the very least, you won't have to tell them all about yourself for a few minutes.

Bottom line: Keep in touch with your parents. Talk to them every couple of days if you're not seeing them that often. They want nothing more for you than to know you're happy and all right. Give them a call, send them an e-mail. At the very least, just let them know you're not dead.

Manipulation

If you've decided to be a conduit, then you know it's a powerful position. If you like, you can choose for yourself what to tell and not to tell each parent. In order to get your way, you could lie and say your mother says one thing and your father says another. It's actually really easy, but that would be a really bad idea. One way or another, your parents will figure out that you're full of it. It's inevitable, because in the end, parents have much better BS detectors than they let on. So when they do find out, which they will, you'll be in the doghouse. Worst of all, after whatever punishments and lectures you receive, you'll have lost their trust.

We'll talk more about stepparents later on, but for now, remember that the same goes for them. Even before they are officially stepparents, they are going to be important figures in your life, whether you like it or not, and it's important to treat them with the same level of respect and trust that you expect from them. It's even harder for stepparents, because they have only known you a short time compared to your parents, friends, and families.

With parents, and actually with everybody, trust ends up

being more valuable than gold. Trust is *especially* valuable with your parents because it's the currency by which you buy your freedom. The more they trust you, the further they'll let you go on your own. But if you lose their trust, you'll end up losing your freedom. So don't try to manipulate your parents. You wouldn't want them to manipulate you.

Reporting

If your parent asks you for a detailed report of everything that's happening at your other parent's house, remind them that you don't work for CNN and that you aren't required to tell them anything. Your parents are separate, their houses are separate, and they should stay that way. This goes back to politics, and it's up to you to decide what's appropriate to share and what isn't. A good guide might be to think about what your parents would share with each other over the phone.

Of course, if something happens at a parent's house that violates Article I of the Divorced Kids' Bill of Rights, then you should definitely say something about it. Your first right is first because it's the most important, and if there is ever anything going on at one of your parent's houses that violates that right, then tell someone immediately. Otherwise, it's no one else's business.

Politics with the World

Yes, divorce is rough. Yes, it might slow you down a little bit at first. Yes, it can be stressful. Yes, people will be sorry that it happened to you. But you know what? You aren't the only one. There are hundreds, thousands, millions of divorces every year. Tens of millions of other kids have gone through something like what you're going through, and unfortunately, a lot of them probably had it worse. But you know what else? They made it. So you probably will too. I hope that makes you feel a little better.

It can be easy to get caught in the trap of using your parents' divorce as an excuse. Like telling your teacher that you forgot your homework at Dad's, or saying that you don't make friends easily because of your parents' divorce. Yes, I have actually heard kids say things like that. But it's really not an excuse, so don't start using it as one. It's not a crutch.

Now, of course, there will be times that you really do forget your homework because it's hard to go from house to house, or you don't see your friends as often as you want to because you're constantly switching back and forth. But the divorce won't cripple you in your life. Only in the most extreme circumstances is divorce that totally debilitating. Yes, it's a challenge, but yes, you can overcome it. Millions have, and I am absolutely positive that you can too.

There is no doubt that any time you are in a group of people your own age, you are going to be around people who have been affected by divorce. Seek them out and talk to them. It's not an excuse to have a pity party, but more so that you know there are people who share your experiences and who might be able to help you out . . . or you can help them out, too.

Part 3

Travel

Traveling on Your Own

Traveling after your parents have been divorced is just like traveling any other time. It can be really fun, but it can also be really stressful. If you're going to be traveling alone from parent to parent, or really for any other reason, it will definitely stress your parents out, if not you. Actually, for the rest of your life, get used to your parents being a bit nervous whenever you travel alone. It doesn't matter if you're seven or seventeen, but when you're in the air, your mom is going to be worrying about you.

When my parents split and my father moved to Colorado, my first visit out to see him was over spring break. My mom knew she didn't have a choice about it, but that didn't stop her from being totally overbearing by wanting to help me pack, triple-checking my bags every fifteen minutes, and just being on a general state of heightened alert.

Know this now: This will happen to you too. There's nothing scarier for a mother than to let her baby (yes, you are her baby) get on a big scary plane that could crash at any moment. It probably didn't help that I was eight years old at the time and I was about to be flying halfway across the country and making a connection in one of the busiest American airports while Colorado was stuck in a snowstorm. Never mind the fact that traveling in a car is much more dangerous than flying—your parents are still liable to freak.

To put my mom—and all those other nervous parents—at ease, whatever airline you end up traveling on will provide you with someone who'll walk you through the airport and stay with you until you get on your flight, and when you land, they'll have someone waiting for you on the other side. This may get annoying if you're twelve and airports are old news, but just deal with it. You'll be flying alone for the rest of your life.

Still, an attendant walking you through the airport can't divert the weather, and sometimes the unexpected will happen. You will miss your connection. You will have to be rerouted. You may have to stay somewhere overnight that isn't your destination. On that first flight, when I landed in Denver two hours late because we were delayed in the air, I was informed that my connection had been canceled, but how would I like to take a four-hour bus ride to Rifle (I thought, *There's a town called Rifle?*), where I could catch a forty-five-minute flight that would put me down around 1 AM?

That was a major pain in the neck. But in the end, it was fine. I was only seven hours late, I had my bag, I was with my dad, and I was ready to explore a new place. So if your flight plans run into some hiccups, please don't freak out about it. You don't have to. There's always another flight, even if it's tomorrow. If things go wrong enough, your airline will give you free stuff like free tickets or upgrades to first class.

Stuck on the plane or in an airport for a while? It's a great opportunity for some quality time: read, do work, or just listen to music, or you can try and make some new friends. Just be careful not to share too much personal information with anyone you don't know. Also, be sure to set an alarm if you like to doze. . . . Sometimes you can sleep right through your boarding announcement!

When it comes time to start arranging your own travel, you have more options than anyone in history. There are tons of websites that look for the cheapest fares, as well as less expensive airlines, which allow you to check in and print your boarding pass at home.

It doesn't matter if you're traveling by bus, train, boat, or camel; in the end, you'll get to your destination. In the end, you'll figure it out, and you won't have to do it alone. Remember, traveling is fun. We all know that it can be stressful, but to help take away that stress, I've made a little checklist of a few essentials for traveling. Take a look at the next section.

The Essential Travel Checklist

☑ Get a cell phone, if you can. They're cheap, they're only getting cheaper, and they're extremely helpful for travel. If something goes wrong, or even if everything goes right, you're going to need to let someone know. If you can't get a cell phone, memorize a few collect numbers, like 1-800-c-a-l-l-a-t-t. You can also always buy a calling card, which will let you call home on the cheap.

If you have a cell phone, *check in*. When you arrive, call everybody who cares (Hint: your mom and dad). They want to know you're safe, so tell them. It's easy. If they're not there, leave a message. All airports have pay phones too, so no matter what, you have no excuse for not letting your parents know you're alive.

Also, if something goes wrong, *let someone know*. Call anyone close by, call both your parents, and if you can't reach them, call someone else. Call your siblings, call your aunts and uncles, call your grandparents, call your friends. If you need help, find someone who can help you.

✓ Before you leave home, find out if you, your family, or your friends know someone in whichever cities you might be traveling through. Write down their numbers, and put them in your cell phone if you have one. But don't rely on your cell phone. Batteries die. Cell phones get lost. When you travel, keep a hard copy of those numbers in your backpack or stuffed into your shoe. You never know how badly you might need them.

✓ Always make sure you have some cash or an ATM card with you in case you need to pay for food, a hotel, a taxi, or any other emergency. Keep half the cash in your wallet, and keep the other half somewhere else. Put it in another pocket, stuff it in your shoe, or hide it in your bag, just in case. Don't carry your wallet in your back pocket. That's just asking for trouble. Carry it up front or in a pocket with a zipper or a button.

✓ Have emergency medical tags. For example, I'm allergic to penicillin, a really common medicine. If I'm alone and passed out, ER techs need to know about my allergy so they don't accidentally kill me. So have a tag on your carry-on bag that gives your name and address, your parents' numbers, and known allergies to food and medications, all that important stuff.

✓ Keep a change of clothes in your carry-on luggage in case your bag doesn't make it. Someday it won't. I was flying through Chicago to meet my mother for a vacation in New

York, and when I missed my connection, my bag went to JFK and they sent me to Newark. I considered myself extremely lucky when I got my bag back, three days later, and I'd wished that I'd had at least a clean pair of socks and a T-shirt for the day it took me to buy a few sets of new clothes. Everyone in smelling distance probably wished that too. No one smells good after eighteen hours of traveling.

☑ Get an iPod, or a laptop, or some books, or else be prepared to sit through sitcom reruns and movies with the fun parts cut out. These days, a lot of the cheap airlines don't even have movies anymore. Your seatmate probably doesn't want to hear your music blasting out of tinny speakers over the drone of the engines, so if you can, buy yourself a nice pair of closed headphones. It's worth it for the quieter trip.

As a side note, when you're blasting your tunes, take a moment to listen when the pilot's talking. Yes, I know, most of the time he's telling you about some fascinating hill or whatever, but once in a while he may actually be talking about delays, connections, or information you'll need to know. So pay attention.

☑ Bring food. Bring lots of food. I don't know about you, but I'm always hungry. Bring sandwiches, bring cookies, bring water or juice, bring whatever you want. It's so much cheaper than buying food at the airport, and besides, airport food either sucks or is too expensive.

☑ Call your parents when you arrive! I know I already said it. I mean it.

☑ The easiest way to make a five-hour trip seem like five minutes is to sleep. I'm all for reading, and an airplane or a train car is a *terrific* place to isolate yourself and get work done. On the other hand, a straight six or seven hours in the same seat, not to mention on coast-to-coast excursions, can be maddening.

I don't sleep very well on planes, so if I'm planning on sleeping, I stay up late the night before, get myself real tired, and by the time I get on the plane, I pass out. (Your parents will probably say this isn't such a good idea. They're probably right.)

☑ Last, double-check. Double-check everything. Double-check your flight time, your arrival time, your flight number, your suitcase, everything. It's always worth a few extra minutes to be prepared.

Emergency Management

Emergencies happen. Your plane will be delayed. Your parents will be late to pick you up. You will hurt yourself. And you might even be the one to see someone else's emergency, and it will be up to you to help.

Now, when most people come to an emergency situation, they do two things: panic, and act immediately—which, of course, are the two absolutely wrong things to do. Panic clouds your judgment and usually causes people to act irrationally. If you act immediately on your panic, you will probably make a situation worse.

Instead, there are three things to do that I think will help anyone make the best decisions in any situation. They are:

1. ASSESS

Take a step back and take a quick look around. See what's going on. Who's involved? How serious is the problem? Who can help?

2. JUDGE

Make some judgments about the situation. Figure out what needs to be done.

3. ACT

Now that you have a handle on what's going on, you can make sensible decisions as to how to act in a way that will help. If you decide this is a situation that's too big for you to handle on your own, immediately seek some help.

For example, you just missed your connection, the plane is gone, and it's not coming back. Instead of freaking out and worrying about all the things that could now go wrong, take a second and think about what's going to have to happen to fix this problem. You're going to need a new flight. To do that you'll have to go to the help desk and let them guide you through it. Think about what information they're going to need, and have it ready. Then call your parents, both of them, and let them know what's happened. Remember, if you sound freaked out, then *they'll* get freaked out. Let me tell you, freaked-out parents are about the worst thing you can have. None of this is rocket science. It's not even jet science. It's just common sense.

Part 4

Your Parents' Relationships and Stepparents

Parental Dating

L ike it or not, your parents probably don't want to stay single forever. And they will date. I know, gross. Believe me, my parents had a few weird boyfriends and girlfriends. But you know what? Most of them were pretty cool. In fact, I still keep in touch with a few of them.

There are two main things to remember when your parents start dating. The first is to always remember your right to feel safe and secure. I can't say it enough times. If your parent ever has someone in his or her life who violates your feelings of safety and security, tell that person or tell your parent. If your parent doesn't take care of it, tell your other parent, tell a counselor, tell everybody, because that's the most important thing.

The other thing to keep in mind is that these boyfriends and girlfriends will come and go. It's more than likely that the first one won't be the right one, and your parents will break up with their girlfriend or boyfriend, just like you do. Weird, right? But that's just how it works. Now that you know that it's likely to happen, don't treat every girlfriend of your dad's like she is your new stepmom, and don't treat every boyfriend your mom has like he is going to be your stepfather.

That doesn't mean you can't get to know them. In all likelihood, they're probably wonderful people. But just know that they might leave someday, and be sensitive to that. Don't tell your dad how much better you liked what's-her-name (his previous girlfriend) in front of his new girlfriend. Stuff like that.

The other possibility, though, is that this new person will become a member of your family for the rest of your life. So try and get to know them, and try to like them. (They desperately want your approval.) Don't wait until the wedding day to try to start a relationship with your new stepmom or stepdad.

An Introduction to Stepparents

Yes, you will probably have stepparents. No, they probably won't be evil. In reality, stepparents can be terrific. They will add a whole new dimension to your family, because they all have families of their own. You'll have new grandparents, new aunts and uncles, new cousins, and maybe even new siblings. Sometimes you may not like these people. It happens. But again, if you like your stepparent, you'll probably like their family too. Sometimes, kids think of stepparents as taking their own parents away from them, but I think that's a limited perspective. Nothing's being taken away. Your family is expanding. If you can't find any way to like them, then at least think of it as a few extra gifts at holiday and birthday times.

If you read my story in the beginning of this book, you know that my father's been married four times, my mother twice, and I have more step—this and—that's than I can count. My brother David said it best when he remarked that sure, anyone can have a nuclear family—Mom, Dad, and a few kids—but not everyone can claim to be living in a postnuclear family.

But stepparents can bring in a whole different set of complications, the first of which is the not-so-simple question of naming. Sometimes a stepparent might want or demand to be called "Mom" or "Dad." If you want to use those names for them, then that's fine—just keep in mind how it might make your *real* mom or dad feel. On the other hand, there was no way I was going to call anyone else mom or dad, so I called my stepparents by their first names. If it doesn't come naturally, just sit down and ask them about it, and try to find an appropriate name for each other. If you don't mind them calling you their child, tell them. If you do, remember that you have the power *and* the responsibility to make it absolutely clear.

Another issue that came up pretty frequently with my stepparents was that strangers would refer to them as my father or mother, and my first impulse would be to immediately say, ahem, "*Step,* actually." But really, the distinction is far more important to you than to strangers, so most of the time, just let it go. So what if they think your stepfather is your father? If it ever really comes up as an issue, then you can correct them. But if it's in passing, then let it pass.

There is something else to keep in mind: the feelings of your other parent. Your father may become jealous or resentful of the position your new stepfather has in your and your mother's lives, or vice versa. This all comes back to politics, and it's important to be sensitive to your parents' feelings. So don't go to your single mom and talk about how in love your father is with your new stepmother or how she tucks you in every single night and that you can talk to her (and not your mom) about all your problems.

Most important, be honest with your parents. If you really like their new choice for a mate, tell them why. If there is one thing that bothers you enough to have doubts about their union, explain that too. Your right to private communication means that you have the right to talk to your mother or father absolutely alone, so that you can be totally honest with them, and not have to worry about anyone else listening in.

Last, don't forget that your right to private communication works with your new stepparents as well. One of the great things that stepparents can do is just be someone who *isn't* your mom and *isn't* your dad. The best ones end up being someone in between—however, more friend than parent.

What Stepparents Can Teach You

Through your stepparents, you will have entire new families of people to get to know. Think of them as more people to help you when you need it, more people you will know around the world. Because of my stepfather, I have friends and family in places like Germany, South Africa, Florida, Toronto, England, France, and tons of other places. Now when I travel, I can go almost anywhere and find someone to stay with or someone to help me if I get stuck. Those are opportunities I'd never have had without my stepparents in my life.

While stepparents can never replace your real parents (and in most circumstances, they are not supposed to), they still have a lot to offer you. Their life experiences may be very different from anyone in your family, and they will have lots they'll want to share with you. Because they come from an outside perspective, they will often see your family in a way that's totally different from the way you, your mother, or your father see it. If you can't figure out why you always get into fights at the dinner table with your mom, your stepdad might be able to clue you in to what was pushing her buttons, and how to apologize. Or even if you are having a problem with someone at school and can't stand the lame advice your parents have given you since you were three, your stepparent might tell you how to deal with it in a new way.

My stepfather taught me that one of the most important time savers in life is the ability to learn from other people's experiences. The more you learn about what other people went through, the more prepared you will eventually be when it's your turn. As more people came into my life, I was able to learn so much from so many perspectives and from so many different parts of life and the world than I ever would have if my parents had stayed together. That advice was a major part of why I wrote this book: so you can shortcut as many of the difficult parts of this experience as you can, and to move you to help other kids do the same by sharing and learning from each other's experiences.

What You Can Teach Your Stepparents

Just like your stepparents probably have a lot they want to teach you or share with you, you have a lot to teach and share with them. You'll probably want to tell them what you like, what kind of music you listen to, what kind of movies you enjoy, or your favorite foods. Sometimes stepparents can joke around and play with you in a way your parents just can't, because the relationships are so different. It's new and different and can be totally awesome.

As you get to know each other, there are a few things you'll have to teach your stepparents, like who you really are as a person or what your study habits are for school. Most important though, you have to teach them boundaries.

Your stepparents may not instinctively recognize what your boundaries are or what is going to make you uncomfortable. Don't expect them to. It's possible that they've never had kids and don't understand how to relate to them. It's possible that they were raised very differently than the way you were. That's okay. But sit down with them, sit down with your parents, and make sure they learn where your boundaries are.

Be sure to let them know if they ever violate those boundaries by mistake—like if your stepparents refer to you as their son or daughter, and you'd prefer they didn't. That's just one example. If they cross your boundaries in any major way, or if they violate that first right, tell them straight out. If they don't stop, tell someone else. You should know the drill by now. And of course, as you get more familiar with each other, these boundaries will probably change. In the end, just give your stepparents a chance. All they want is for you to like them, and eventually maybe you'll even come around to loving them.

Part 5

Your Support System

Building a Support System

You're probably getting tired of hearing it, and frankly I'm getting a little tired of saying it, but it's so important that I really can't say it enough: Find someone to talk to. There are all sorts of people out there who are ready to listen and help you if you need it. The world is full of people who care, as hard as that is to see or believe sometimes.

At first it was tough for me to even *want* to talk to other people about my problems. I kept telling myself that I was strong enough to do this on my own, I would be weak going to someone else for help, I didn't need anyone, blah blah blah. That was stupid. Other people are there, ready to help, and refusing help is only going to end up making things more difficult and overwhelming.

But don't go unloading your life story and your deepest darkest emotional secrets to someone just because they ask how you're feeling. A few close friends you can tell anything to will make more of an impact in your life than a thousand acquaintances ever could. Sometimes we just need some good advice and an outside perspective, so be open to it. Find the right people, and try to be that person for others too.

Support from Friends of the Family

It's hard to find someone to talk to because you don't know whom to trust, and it's important to know that you can't trust everybody. Friends of your parents can be good, because they can offer some insight and they see the whole process from a different perspective. The danger there, however, is that sometimes these friends have an allegiance with one parent over the other, and they aren't exactly unbiased. So make sure you know how those people feel about the whole situation. It can be difficult to know how much they'll actually keep secret. Don't assume they won't repeat what you say to your parents.

Friends of the family can be a terrific resource despite all these warnings. They often have a unique perspective or may know something about a situation that you don't, and if they know your parent or parents well, then they can offer very good, specific advice. They can be extremely helpful in presenting information to your parents in a way they'd want to hear it, or they can even find out information for you that your parents won't necessarily tell you.

In fact, it's pretty likely that some of your parents' friends will have known them longer than you've been alive, and may have even known your parents when they were your age. They'll be able to tell you all kinds of things about your parents that you'd never otherwise know, and sometimes they can help you understand your parents' actions and feelings. In the end, just make sure you don't start any wars, step on anyone's toes, or burden someone with secrets they aren't ready to hear.

Support from Relatives

Your siblings, if you have any, can be a great source for support. I have three older brothers who all went through a divorce before I did, and they had a lot of valuable information to share. They also had a lot of perspective on my mother and father as people, and they helped me get new perspectives on my situation. The great thing about family is that they can be really good at keeping secrets. And don't forget your grandparents, aunts, uncles, and cousins. They all care about you and will listen to you.

If it happens that you're the oldest sibling, then you'd better know that your younger siblings will need you more than ever. This is probably even harder for them, and you will be their best resource by far. All the help and advice you're looking for, they are also looking for in you. So just remember that they need you, and do your best to help them however you can.

It's also possible, even likely, that you may have new stepbrothers or stepsisters. Throwing two families together is a tricky proposition, and no one expects everyone to get along instantly. Keep in mind that your new stepsiblings are probably going through a lot of the same issues you are and can offer you a whole host of new perspectives the same way your stepparents can. Do your best to be open to them, and welcome them into your family. (It's not like you really get a choice, right?) Of course, if you *do* have a serious problem with one of your new siblings, then by now you should know how to take care of it.

Other good relatives to talk to can be your grandparents, who have an entire lifetime of experience to draw from. They see things from an entirely different perspective and can give you a lot of insight into the behavior of their children (your parents). Just keep in mind that they can also be just as biased as anyone else, perhaps even more so when the subject is about their daughter or son. Don't forget, you also have aunts, uncles, cousins, and all of your new "steps" as well.

Support from the Outside

By the outside, I mean counselors or people in whatever religious organization or social services group you may be a part of. These people are often trained to help you and have seen this kind of thing before, probably many times. They are great people to go to for advice, or when you need to get stuff off your chest. These people will do everything they can to make sure that you feel safe and secure at all times. You can find them at your school—just tell your teacher you want to talk to someone. Most schools, if not all of them, have a counseling department, and they are there for you.

These are the best people to talk with when you're feeling emotions you can't understand, or you're feeling guilt, anger, confusion, or depression, and you don't have siblings to ask for advice. Remember, these people can empower you and help you make your voice heard. If there's something you're trying to tell your parents and they aren't hearing you, then your counselor can be your voice and make them listen.

Support from Other Kids Like You

You aren't the only kid going through this, and I'm sure that statement doesn't come as a surprise. There are kids in your classes, on your block, and everywhere else who have gone through or are going through a divorce. They can be great people to make friends with, or compare notes with, and you can help each other get through it all. It's always great to find help from people in your peer group, because they can more easily see your perspective. Once you know how to deal with this whole thing, if you want to, you can help other kids in your community. If you're out there looking for them, they're out there looking for you too. At the very least, be an open and nonjudgmental ear for your peers and friends.

Part 6

Heading Toward the Bright Side

The Good News and the Bad News

Everyone's going to be telling you, "Oh, divorce is great, divorce is fine, it's all going to be okay, your life will be better," and all kinds of other platitudes. In fact, that's exactly what I've been saying for most of this book so far, and I've been telling you that because it's true. Divorce can be awesome. Really. I'd honestly say that my parents' divorce is one of the best things to ever happen to me in my entire life: That's the good news.

On the other hand, divorce can make you wake up one morning realizing how much everything just *sucks*. There are times I've wished more than anything that my parents could have just sat down and worked out their own problems and stayed married, and I dream about what my life could be like, then I mope because it isn't that way and because they're stressed out about arguing over who's going to pay my tuition bill. Believe me, I've had plenty of those days: That's the bad news.

Normally I'd ask you which one you want to hear first, but since you don't really have a choice (unless you skip ahead), I'll start with the bad news.

The Downside

You Are Never Going to Have One Home Again

Your stuff will never be in one place. *You* will never be in one place. You're going to ask yourself, a lot, "Did I leave that at Dad's house?" and the answer from Mom will be "Yes, you did. Why can't you be more responsible, why exactly do I have to drive you to your father's house at a quarter to midnight again, and is it really that important?" Or maybe you'll just be told to deal with it. Either way, it's going to happen.

But it also means that if your parents live close enough, you've always got somewhere else to go. Having a fight with your dad? You don't have to stay there. Little stepsister won't stop asking "Why, why, why, why, why?" Go relax somewhere else. It's nice to be able to get out and gain a new perspective whenever you want it, and that's a luxury that you have.

Of course, you may have a different situation where you're spending most or all of your time with one parent in one house. If that's the case, then relax—you're going to have a much easier time keeping organized and keeping track of your schoolwork, books, and other stuff. And since you might not have the option that other divorced kids have of switching houses, take some time to find a place that's safe and quiet where you can work or relax, like a local school library, for those times you just need to escape for a few hours.

The Downside

Your Parents Are Going to Fight

I guess this is kind of a given. Your parents are getting divorced because they don't see the world or each other the same way anymore. Their biggest fights are probably going to be about you. It sucks when people you love can't get along, especially when they're fighting about you. All you want is for them to stop. They won't. At least, there is nothing you can do to make them.

Their fights are their own, and by far the best thing you can do is stay out of the way. Get out of earshot, don't listen, and never, ever, ever get involved. If they try to get you to take a side, demand they stop. When the fight is over, do your best to leave the whole subject alone. If your parent tries to explain what the fight was about, feel free to listen, silently. You aren't there to tell them they're right.

I'll tell you what: they would have fought anyway, divorced or not. Ask your friends whose parents are still together, they'll tell you. No one's parents get along perfectly 100 percent of the time. No one. Besides, it's a lot easier to deal with your parents' fighting after they're divorced. They'll probably fight less, and they won't have to be in the same house with each other afterward. So that's not so bad either.

74

The Downside

You May Learn Things About Your Parents You Didn't *Ever* Want to Know

This may or may not happen, but be prepared if it does. You will most likely, at some point, hear from your mother the reasons she divorced your father. And you'll hear from your father the reasons he divorced your mother. They will say things about each other, whether you want them to or not, that aren't going to be very nice. So if you thought your parents were perfect, divorce is an express ticket to the real world, where real people have real problems, and even real flaws. I'm not saying that your parents aren't wonderful people with all of the great qualities that you see in them, and probably more. Up to now, they've been your parents, and you were their kid and you saw them through those eyes. But be prepared for your perspective to change when you start to see them through the eyes of one another, because sometimes you'll see things in each of your parents that make them less than perfect.

But in reality, you already knew that your parents weren't perfect, because no one is. The flip side is that the better you know your parents, the better you can deal with them. Most teenagers experience all sorts of arguments and fights with their parents as they go through adolescence, and a lot of the time it's because they're realizing that their parents are people, just like them and everyone else. So the sooner you can know that, and accept and love them and know their best qualities *and* flaws, the easier it'll be for you to get along with them during those difficult years.

I also wanted to share a little tidbit of parental behavior that I've learned through this whole process. My parents rarely ever get angry with me, because I do my best not to make them mad. After a while, I learned better and better what would set them off. Whenever I started acting in a way that reminded one of my parents about why they fought with the other, it opened some very deep wounds, and that anger or loss or frustration would come pouring out directly at me. I don't even think they realized they were doing it.

For example, if my father thinks I'm being manipulative, he associates that with my mother and gets angry. By that same token, if my mother thinks I am being arrogant, she associates that trait with my father and she blows her top. So now I know why my parents get angry with me, and how to avoid it, which is a useful skill in any household.

The Downside

You Will Probably Move More Often

I'll say it flat out—moving sucks. Every time you move, you have to pack everything up, and things inevitably get broken or lost. When you move in to your new house, you're going to have to get used to a new neighborhood, new neighbors, maybe a new school, and maybe new weather, depending on how far you move. It's always hard to start feeling at home in a new house, and for your new room to feel familiar.

Here comes the counterpoint: I actually find moving, for all its hassle and frustration, to be a cleansing experience. Stick with me here. Every time I move, it makes it a lot easier to get rid of all the junk that just builds up and up and up. Things become less dear to you when you think about schlepping them across the country. Plus, I love exploring new places and seeing new things. Maybe it's in my nature, or maybe I've become that way because I moved so much. Thinking about it, I realized that I've called at least seventeen different places my room in seventeen different houses in the last nineteen years. I know that's a little extreme, and I wouldn't wish that on anybody, but moving isn't *all* bad.

The worst parts of moving always are separating from your

friends and your school. When I moved from Los Angeles to San Francisco, I had to leave my entire group of childhood friends behind. And when I got to my new school, I was the biggest social outcast you ever saw. It happens. It's hard to be the new kid. New schools have new rules, new customs, new cliques, new bullies, new teachers, new subjects, new everything. It's a lot to deal with all at once, but lots of people do it. We've all had new kids in our class at some point, and now maybe it's your turn. The bottom line is just to be confident in yourself, and people will respect you for it.

The other thing that's tough is losing old friends. Moving away means you won't see them very often, if at all. More bad news: you're going to lose touch with some of them, but that's really okay. The thing is, the friends who really care about you won't care how far away you are. You'll stay friends. Those other friends of convenience will fade away, and you'll be left with the friends who really matter.

The Downside

Your Parents Will Lose Friends

Don't forget, you're not the only one moving around here. You're not even going through a divorce, so consider yourself lucky. Your parents may be moving away from their friends too, and in some cases, some of your parents' friends will side with one parent or the other. It's hard to be a loyal friend to two people who can't stand each other anymore, and sometimes your mom or dad might feel betrayed by their formerly close friends. It can be easy to get yourself caught in the middle, but remember that your relationships with these people concern you, not your parents. Their loyalties to one parent or the other shouldn't affect their friendship with you.

So just be aware, keep your eyes open. Your parents will probably be lonely sometimes. Remember that you are the most important person in the world to them, and you can comfort them better than anyone else can.

The Downside

Your Parents Will Have Less Money

Divorces aren't cheap. Lawyers aren't cheap. Supporting yourself and your child or children alone isn't cheap. Your parents may have less money for a while during and after the divorce. There's nothing you can do about it, so don't *worry* about it. Just know that it's going on.

Having less money makes a lot of things a little more difficult. Be aware of it, and don't pout if they don't buy you a new bike for Christmas. Or when they take you shopping for new school clothes, stay out of Abercrombie and check out the sale rack. Other consequences might also come from your parents' new financial situation. You may have to share a room with your siblings, whereas you had your own room before. You may move out of a house and into an apartment.

In the end, the only way to make it easier is to be understanding. Fighting these changes will only serve to make everyone more unhappy. Your parents are going through a lot, so do what you can to help. They'll appreciate it more than you know. The other thing is that it won't last forever. Know that your parents are trying, and do your best to make it easier on all of you.

So that's the bad news. And it wasn't so bad, was it?

One last thing: Ever heard the saying, "There are no bad experiences"? If you hadn't, well, now you have. I'm not saying that it's absolutely the truth, and I don't want to get into those bad experiences here. What I'm trying to say is that most experiences, even most of the bad ones, can either hurt you forever or end up teaching you a lot about yourself and other people; they can even teach you how to be a better and more successful person.

What makes the difference? You do. It's all about how you take it and how you look at things. Take a step back and consider the bigger picture once in a while. Think about how it's all going to play out. Maybe you'll see that the bad news really isn't so bad after all.

The Bright Side

You Will See More New Places

When your parents split, it's possible that one of them will move to a new city or state. And while that can be difficult to deal with at first, it brings with it thousands of new experiences.

If my parents hadn't divorced, I would have never known about Aspen, Colorado. I would never have learned to ski. I would never have learned to travel by myself at eight years old. I would never have had the opportunity to explore Colorado with my father. I'd have never lived in an apartment in the middle of a major city. I probably would have never ended up going to boarding school. Maybe I'd have never even moved up to San Francisco. All these experiences have greatly affected my life, and I'm thankful for them every day. I wouldn't trade them for anything.

Also, realize that it's a unique opportunity to travel and explore with a single parent, and it can greatly change and strengthen your relationship. Most kids are outside of the decision-making circle or are just along for the ride while their parents travel together. Parents will always be parents, but it's those kinds of situations that can allow you and your parents to be friends as well as family.

The Bright Side

You Will Have More Independence

Because your parents will have to spend more time worrying about themselves, they'll have less time to spend worrying about and taking care of you. I don't mean this to sound like bad news. What I mean is, since they can't take care of you all the time, you'll get to start taking care of yourself.

You will be listened to more often. Your parents want to make sure that everything is all right with you, that you are okay. This can give you an opportunity you wouldn't have otherwise to have your voice heard and to have your opinion matter.

While your parents are trying to support themselves, it's likely that you will have more time alone, whether that time is outside and around town or in your house. You can learn to cook. You can learn to use public transportation. You can learn how to do laundry and run a house. It's a few steps closer to living life like an adult.

I'll let you in on a little secret: most kids have no idea how to do any of these things. And I'm not just talking about eight-year-old kids. I'm talking about eighteen-year-old kids too. In fact, there are plenty of adults who can't figure this stuff out because they never learned it when they were young. Speaking from personal experience, it's a really nice thing to be able to take care of yourself and not to have to depend on anyone else.

Two things come from independence: freedom and responsibility. It takes a lot of kids a long time to be able to handle those things. For you, if you are up to the challenge, you'll be years ahead of your peers. Who doesn't like a head start?

The Bright Side

You Will Learn How to Fly

When I went to boarding school, I was sixteen. I got off a plane with lots of other kids, and half of them were freaking out. Their moms had packed their luggage; they didn't know where to pick it up or what to do. They had never flown alone. In all likelihood, you probably won't choose to go to boarding school, and you may never even have to travel by yourself until you've graduated from high school. But if you do, consider yourself lucky, and use it as an opportunity to get a leg up on people who don't know how travel alone.

It's nice to be able to fly and get around on your own. It makes everything much easier. As the child of divorced parents, you'll learn fast how to pack your own bags and how to choose your own flights. The more responsibility you take on for yourself, the easier it all gets.

The Bright Side

You Will Meet a Lot of New People

Stepparents. Stepcousins. Stepaunts and stepuncles. New friends, new neighbors, strangers on airplanes. Suddenly, you'll find that the circle of people you knew when your parents were together has grown exponentially. The benefits that come with meeting new people are too numerous to name, but I'll give it a shot.

Thanks to my ever-extending network of family and friends, I have contacts in hundreds of places around the world. My grandmother lives in Las Vegas. My stepgrandmother lives in L.A. I have stepcousins in Toronto. My brother's mother has a brother in Paris. My stepfather has friends in London. I have a second cousin in Florida, and more family in Baltimore, Seattle, Washington D.C., New York, Ohio, and Texas. It's reassuring and makes life easier to have safety and support nets of family and friends all over the world, in places I've never even been yet. All these people from all over the world can open your eyes to new cultures and ways of life, and you'll find yourself knowing a lot more about the world than many of your peers who've never lived in a different city. With all these new people you can connect to, who knows where you'll find your next relative? You may have the opportunity to visit any number of places in the world, and even have someone with whom you can stay.

The Bright Side

You Can Become a Resource and a Mentor for Other Kids

Your mission, should you choose to accept it, is to help other kids through this stuff too. Thousands of marriages end every day, and a lot of those marriages involve kids just like you, and just like me. You know them. They're in your classes at school, they attend your church or synagogue. You play soccer or baseball with them. A lot of them have no idea how to deal with it. They're looking for someone to talk to, and more than anything, they need someone who understands.

I was lucky. My parents and lots of people around me helped me figure a lot of this out, and I found help when I was young. You have this book, and chances are your parents are helping you a lot too. But many of these kids don't have this book, and their parents aren't helping them the same way. It's for kids like these that divorce really does become the worst thing that's ever happened in their lives. So if you want to, you can help. Find them, talk to them. A lot of kids might not want to talk about it, and you shouldn't force anyone to. I wouldn't want you to go around seeking out kids going through difficult divorces and demand that they share their life story with you—but if it comes up, then you're going to have a lot of useful things to tell them and advice to give.

Tell them that seeing a counselor isn't lame or useless. Explain that they aren't alone in this, and that it's not the end of the world, but rather a whole new set of opportunities to take advantage of. Remember, though, that you might end up hearing something bigger than you can handle, and it's up to you to use that information wisely. You don't want to betray anyone's trust, but if there is the potential for real danger, physical or otherwise, then you have a responsibility to make sure that person is safe. So don't try to save the world, but at least make it clear, if you want to, that you can offer a helping hand. Make yourself a new friend, and help someone. They'll thank you for it.

The Bright Side

You Will Gain Insight into Relationships Between People

While watching my parents get divorced, I realized: This is the last thing I want to do when I grow up. I observed as my parents, two people who'd loved each other enough to raise me and stay married for ten years, had their marriage disintegrate into screaming matches and custody battles. I asked myself over and over again: How could this have happened? How could these two people who loved each other suddenly stop?

Ever since then, I've tried to figure out what makes a successful relationship work and what makes a successful relationship fall apart. I look at my parents to see what it was in each other that drove them apart. Sometimes I find personality traits in my parents that I don't like, which is never fun, but from that point on I do my best to never act in the same way. Watching my parents' divorce and subsequent remarriages, it seems that some of the most essential qualities for a successful relationship include complete trust, totally open and honest communication, and a willingness to listen and compromise. While getting married is easy, and staying married isn't much harder, staying married *and happy* seems to be all too rare these days. Perhaps the best thing that a divorce can teach you is more about who you are and about the reasons a relationship can either work or fall apart.

Epilogue: It's Over!

One more piece of good news: This is the end. You made it! Like I've said before, there are tons of people who'll tell you that divorce is the most traumatizing and horrible thing that can ever happen to a child. I don't think it's true, and I hope that after reading this book, you agree with me. Looking back on what I've learned about my parents, the world, and myself, I would say that my parents' divorce was one of the best things that ever happened to me. I know that might not be true for everyone. But I hope this book can help make that statement true for you too.

Ok, I lied. I have to tell you one last thing, the truest advice my mother ever gave me: Our characters and our lives are distinguished not by what happens to us, but by how we *keep responding* to what happens to us. From now on and forever, unexpected, stressful events will come to pass and things will rarely go the way you hoped or planned. But distinguish yourself by reacting to situations the best that you can by rising above it and by learning from every experience.

Thanks for reading all the way through. I hope this helps you realize that it's up to you to make this experience into a good one and that you have the power to do so.

BT 11/5/07

Index